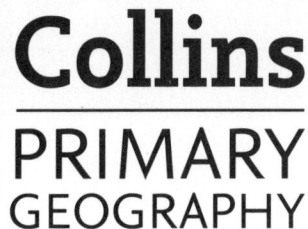

World around me
Workbook 1

Planet Earth	Air	2
	Water	4
	Soil	6
	Rock	8
Weather	Sun	10
	Rain	12
	Cold	14
	Wind	16
Local area	Home	18
	Shops	20
	School	22
	Park	24
Food and farming	Vegetables	26
	Fruit	28
	Bread	30
	Milk	32
Habitats	Woods	34
	Grass	36
	Sand	38
	Ponds	40
Journeys	Walking	42
	Wheels	44
	Cars and lorries	46
	Buses and trains	48
Mapwork skills	Colour	50
	Near and far	52
	Low and high	54
	Signs	56
Maps and plans	Maps and plans	58
	Our world	60

Daphne Paizee

Air

Air is all around us

1 Yes or no? Are they blowing air? Colour the answer.

Yes   No

Yes   No

Yes   No

Yes   No

Things float in the air

❷ Where is the air? Colour the air blue.

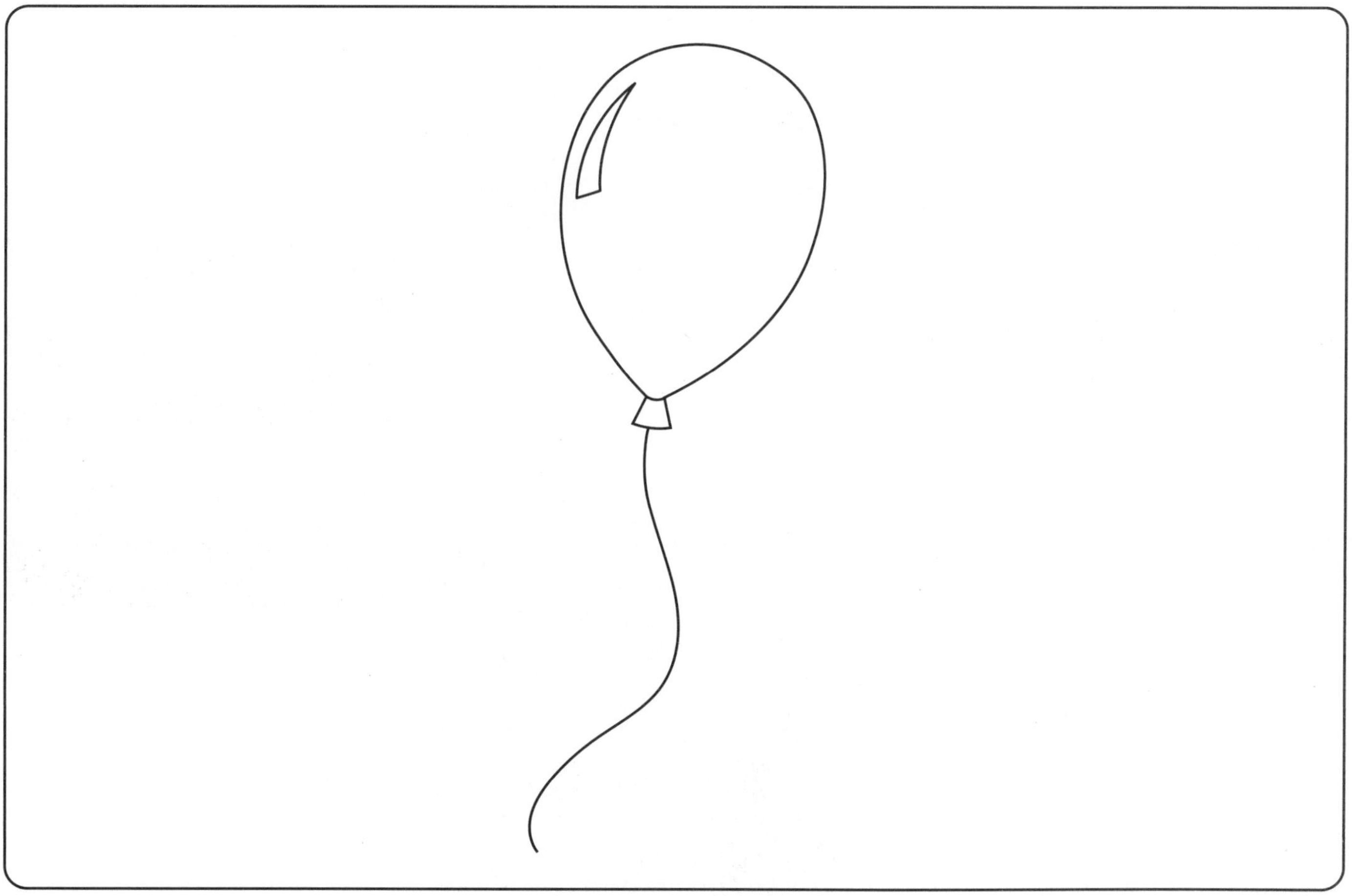

Water

The world is full of water

1 We can see water. Draw lines to match the words to the pictures.

river

waterfall

clouds

puddle

tap

pond

We can use water

❷ How do you use water? Draw a picture.

Soil

The ground is made of soil

1 Circle five words in the puzzle. They all need soil.

mole

worm

bird

x	b	b	j	p
s	k	i	y	l
w	o	r	m	a
m	q	d	o	n
h	z	g	l	t
t	r	e	e	j

tree

plant

Living things need soil

2 Draw on the picture:
- 2 worms
- 1 bird
- 3 plants
- 1 tree

Rock

Rock makes solid ground

1 Look at the pictures. Circle the odd one out.

Soft or hard?

rocks · sand · pebbles

Soft or hard?

pebbles · mud · sand

Soft or hard?

water · pebbles · boulders

Rocks are different shapes and sizes

❷ Complete the picture of the beach.
Colour the sand.
Draw some rocks and pebbles.

❸ Write the words on your picture.

rocks   sand   pebbles

Sun

The sun is very hot

❶ What do you do on a sunny day?
Draw a picture.

The sun is a ball of fire in space

❷ Write the words on the picture.

sun   moon   Earth

❸ Complete the sentence.

We need the _____ to live. It gives us light and warmth.

Rain

Rain falls from the sky

1 What do you wear when it rains?

Complete the picture.

Rain falls from the sky

Wet weather changes

2 Yes or no? Colour the answer.

   a) A drizzle is a light rain.

Yes   No

   b) The rain is gentle in a storm.

Yes   No

   c) A rain shower lasts for a short time.

Yes   No

Cold

Cold weather changes what we do

❶ Draw a picture of cold weather where you live. What can you do outside?

Cold weather freezes rain

❷ Colour the cold weather words.

- snow
- rain
- ice
- frost
- sunny
- icicle
- cold
- stones

Wind

Wind changes the weather

❶ Write the words on the map of the United Kingdom.

north   south   east   west

❷ Circle the words about the wind in the United Kingdom.

The North Wind makes the weather …

cold   hot

The West Wind makes the weather …

rainy   sunny

The wind moves and blows

❸ Wind is not always the same. Draw a picture of the wind each day.
Circle a word about the wind.

Day 1	[flag hanging straight down]	breeze (still) gale
Day 2		breeze still gale
Day 3		breeze still gale
Day 4		breeze still gale
Day 5		breeze still gale

Home

Home has the things we need

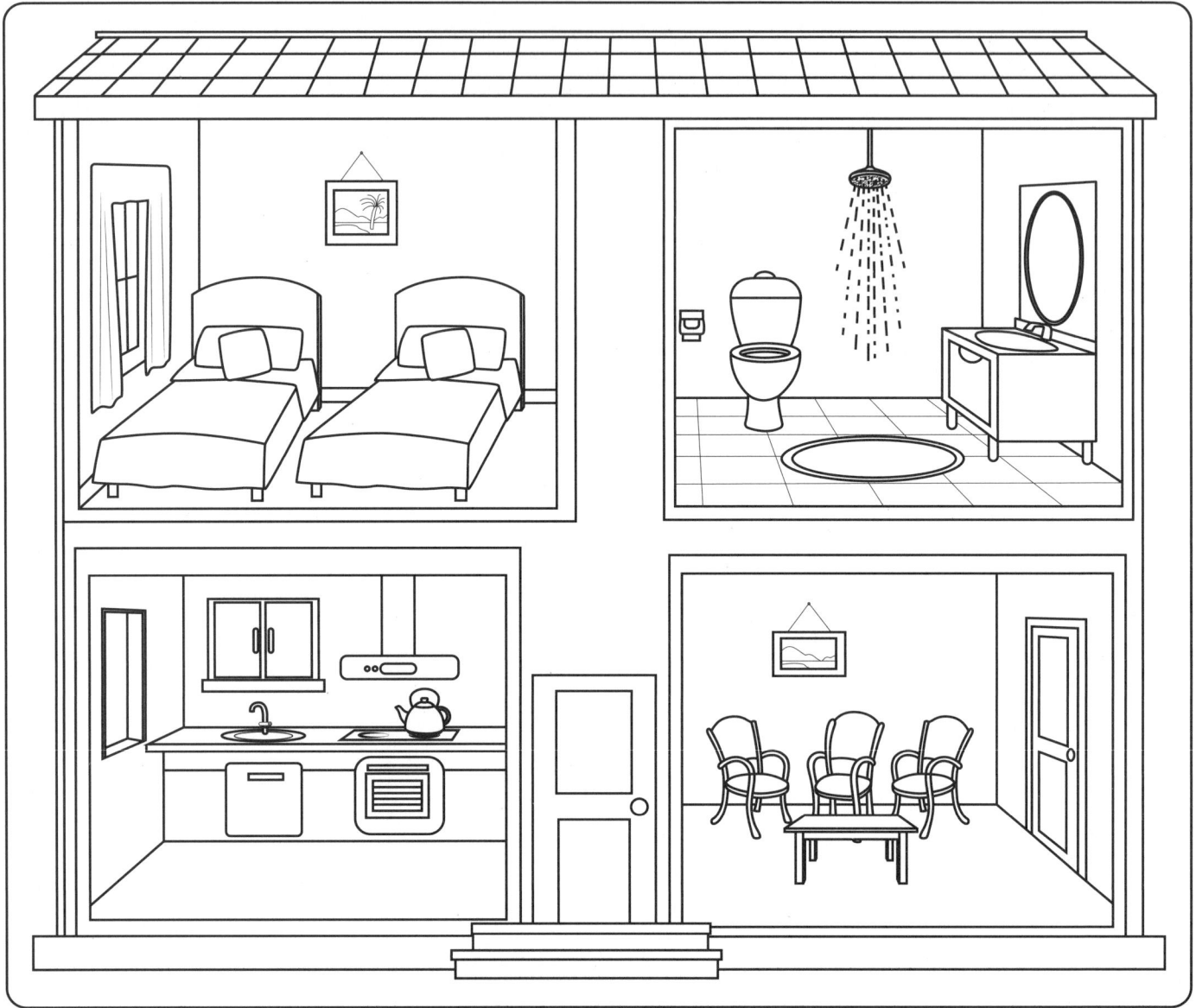

1 Circle the best word.

There are [**four**] [**two**] 🛏 beds in the bedroom.

There are [**two**] [**three**] 🪑 chairs in the living room.

The 🚽 toilet is in the [**kitchen**] [**bathroom**].

The 🫖 pot is in the [**kitchen**] [**bathroom**].

We use places in the home

❷ We can do jobs at home. Tick ✓ the correct sentence.

a)
- ☐ He is sleeping in a bedroom.
- ☐ He is cooking in the kitchen.

b)
- ☐ They are helping in the kitchen.
- ☐ They are helping in the bathroom.

c)
- ☐ They are playing in the living room.
- ☐ They are washing in the living room.

Shops

Shops sell the things we need

❶ What do you buy from shops? Draw pictures.

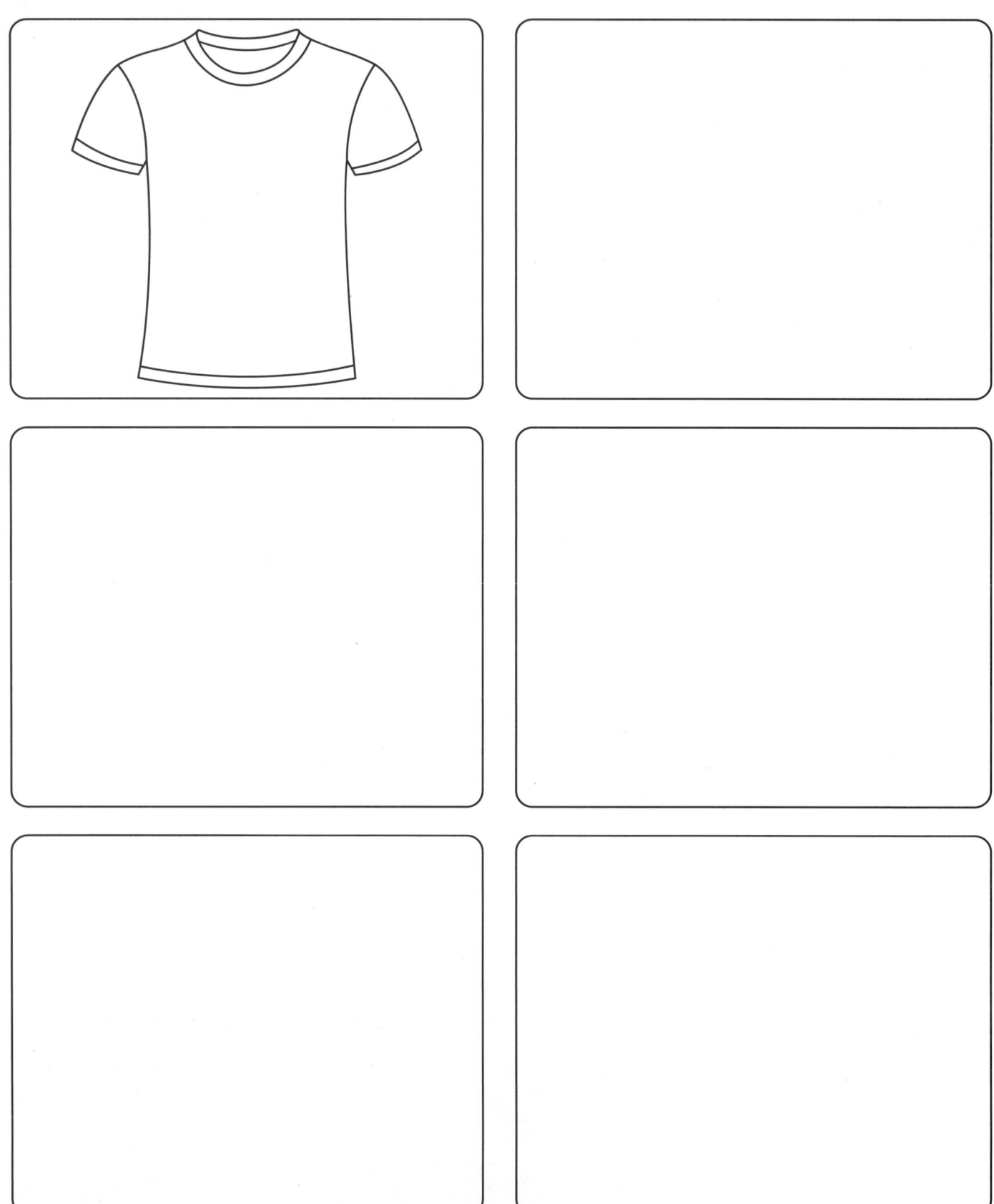

Shops are not the same

❷ Draw lines to match the things to the shops.

- fruit
- shoes
- toys
- furniture
- books
- bread

School

Schools help us to learn

❶ What do you do at school? Tick ✓ the words.

play ✓	paint ☐	count ☐
write ☐	sleep ☐	eat ☐
run ☐	read ☐	

22

There are places and spaces in a school

❷ Colour in the key with one colour for each place.

Key

playground	
classroom	
hall	
cloakroom	

❸ Colour in the places in a school. Use the colours in the key.

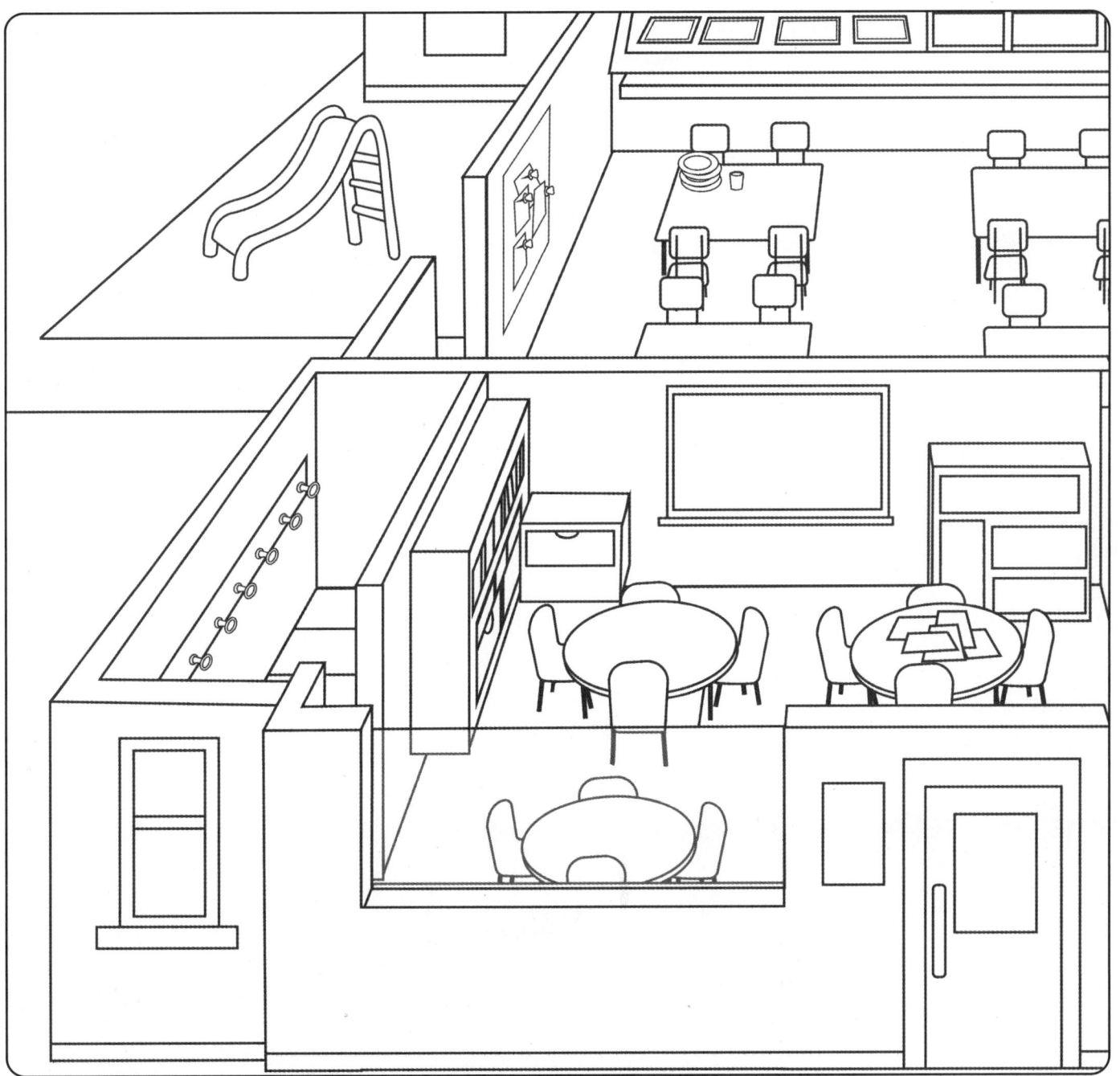

Park

Parks are fun and healthy

1 Are the parks the same? Circle six differences.

We can do lots of things in a park

❷ Look at page 27 of your Pupil Book.
Draw all the things you see.

Vegetables

Vegetables help our bodies to grow

❶ Circle the vegetables.

❷ Circle the names of six vegetables in the word snake. One has been done for you.

x c ⓞⓝⓘⓞⓝ k l b e a n s z l c a b b a g e q r p u m p k i n k h c a r r o t k z p o t a t o

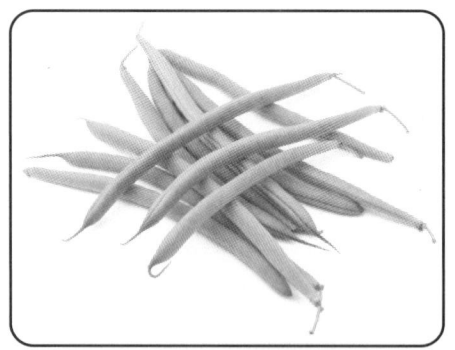

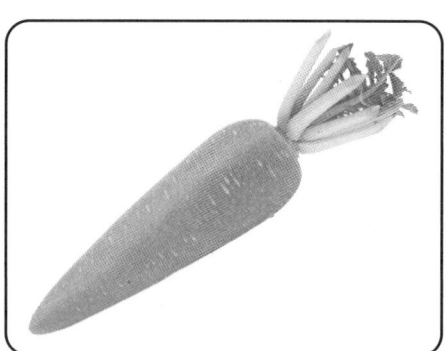

Farmers grow vegetables

❸ Tick ✓ yes or no.

	Yes	No
Vegetables grow in the air.		✓
Farmers grow vegetables.		
Carrots are fruit.		
Cabbages are vegetables.		
Vegetables help us grow.		
Beans can be long and green.		

❹ Draw a vegetable that you like. Write the name.

_____

Fruit

Fruit is sweet and healthy

1 What time of the year is it? Circle the word.

spring   winter   autumn   summer

2 Write the names of the parts of an apple.

leaf   skin   core   seeds   stalk

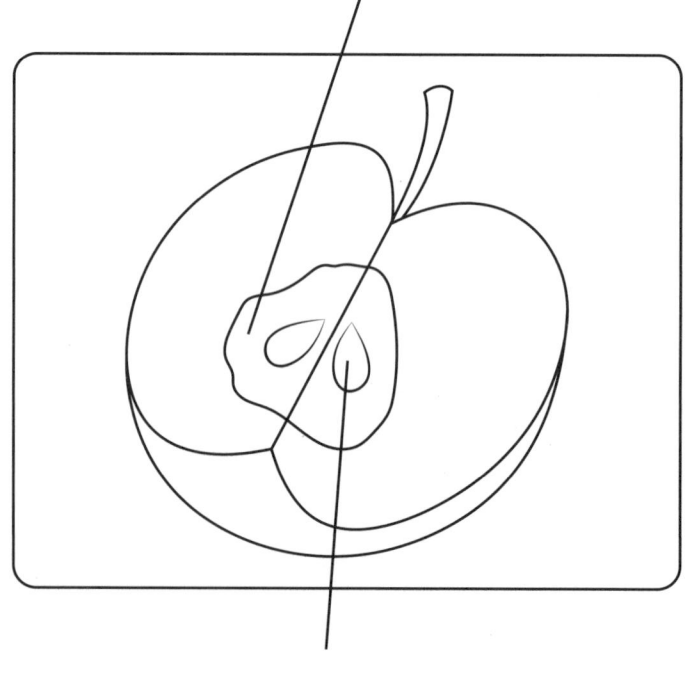

There are different kinds of fruit

❸ Draw lines to match the words to the pictures.

plum

grapes

pear

orange

banana

❹ Draw a fruit that you like. Write the name.

29

Bread

Bread is made from seeds

1 Put the pictures in the right order. Write the numbers.

We can make bread

② Draw different breads.

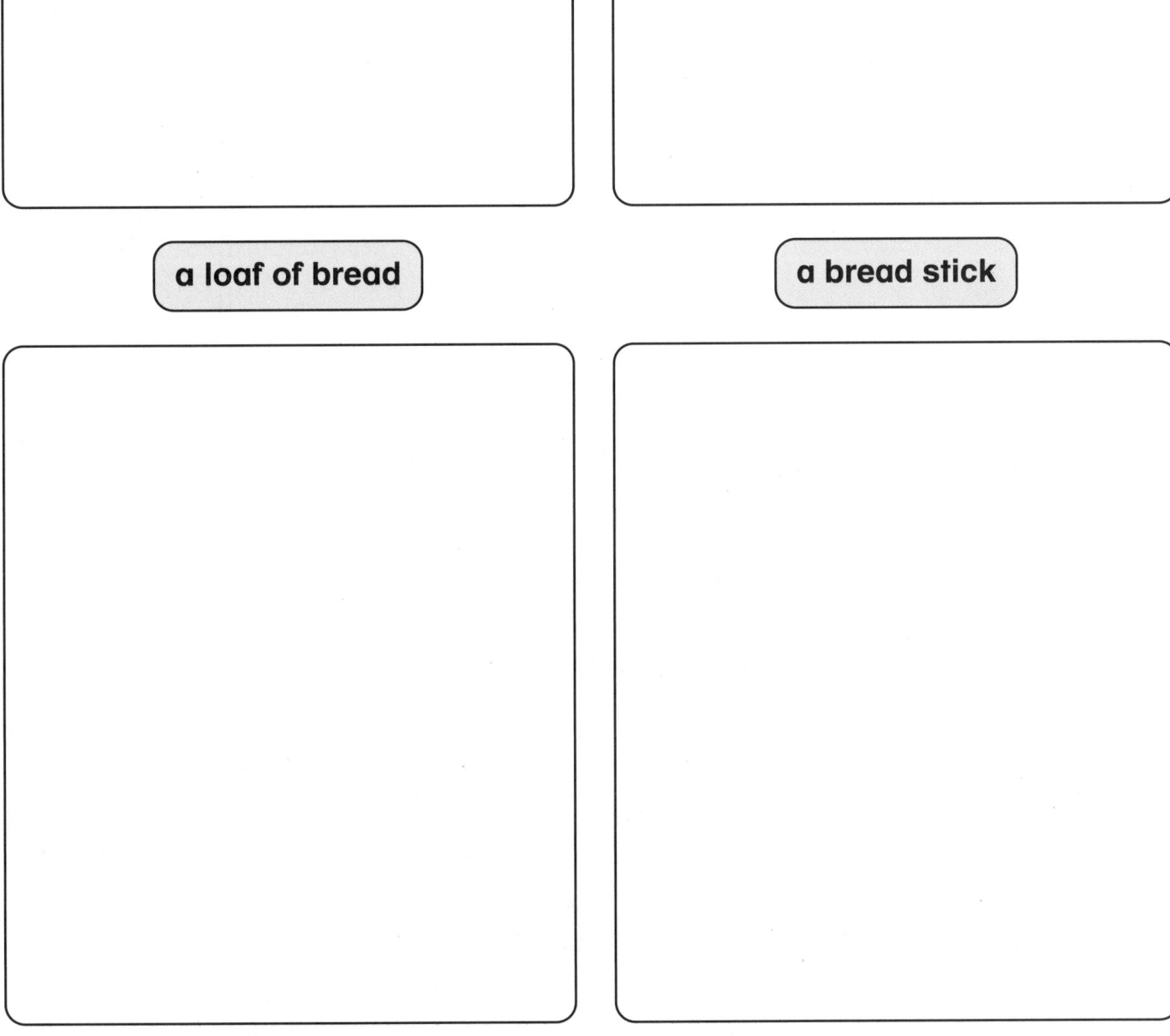

a loaf of bread

a bread stick

a flat bread

a bagel

31

Milk

Milk is drink and food

1 Circle the foods made with milk.

Milk comes from cows

Milk comes from cows. It also comes from goats and water buffalo.

② a) Draw lines to match the words to the pictures.

water buffalo   cow   goat

b) What other animals give us milk?

_____

Other food is made from milk

③ What food do you eat that comes from milk? Draw a picture.

Woods

Woods are shady places

1 Find 10 plants and animals that live in the woods. Circle the words in the puzzle.

s	q	u	i	r	r	e	l	w	x
n	k	p	a	a	d	o	h	z	t
a	f	q	s	b	a	d	g	e	r
k	o	l	y	b	w	p	j	n	e
e	x	d	b	i	r	d	p	l	e
k	v	g	e	t	c	e	q	j	m
b	s	c	a	y	h	e	r	f	j
b	z	r	r	n	x	r	r	g	i
t	o	a	d	s	t	o	o	l	z

The wood is a home

2 Tick ✓ yes or no.

	Yes	No
The wood is a home for plants and animals.	✓	
There is water in the woods.		
A badger lives in a hole.		
It is good to cut down trees.		

3 Draw an animal or plant that lives in a wood. Write the name.

_____

Grass

Grass makes open spaces

1 Read the story. Complete the picture.

Tom sits on the grass.
The grass is green.
Ants take his bread.
Snails take his lettuce.
No more food for Tom!

Grass is a home

2 Look at page 39 of your Pupil Book. How many creatures are in the picture? Draw pictures. Write the number.

butterfly		5
worm		
slug		
ant		
snail		

Sand

The seashore is a changing place

1 Are the seashores the same? (Circle) six differences.

A sandy shore is a home

❷ Work out the names of the creatures that live on the shore. Draw pictures.

| llug | _gull_ | barc | _____ |

| malc | _____ | wormlug | _____ |

Ponds

Ponds are a water habitat

❶ Circle the best word.

A pond has **water** **waves** in it.

A place where creatures live is called a **habit** **habitat**.

Fish **Ducks** swim on the water.

Fish live **under** **above** the water.

❷ Write about the picture.

_____

_____

A pond is a home

❸ Tidy the pond. Draw a picture of the pond without rubbish.

❹ Circle the things that live in a pond.

frogs   cats   ducks   fish   cows   plants   bears

Walking

Walking is for short journeys

1 Where are they walking? Draw lines to match the places to the pictures.

across the road

on a footpath

on the pavement

on the sand

42

We can walk to places

2 Pip wants to go to the library. Colour in the path to the library.

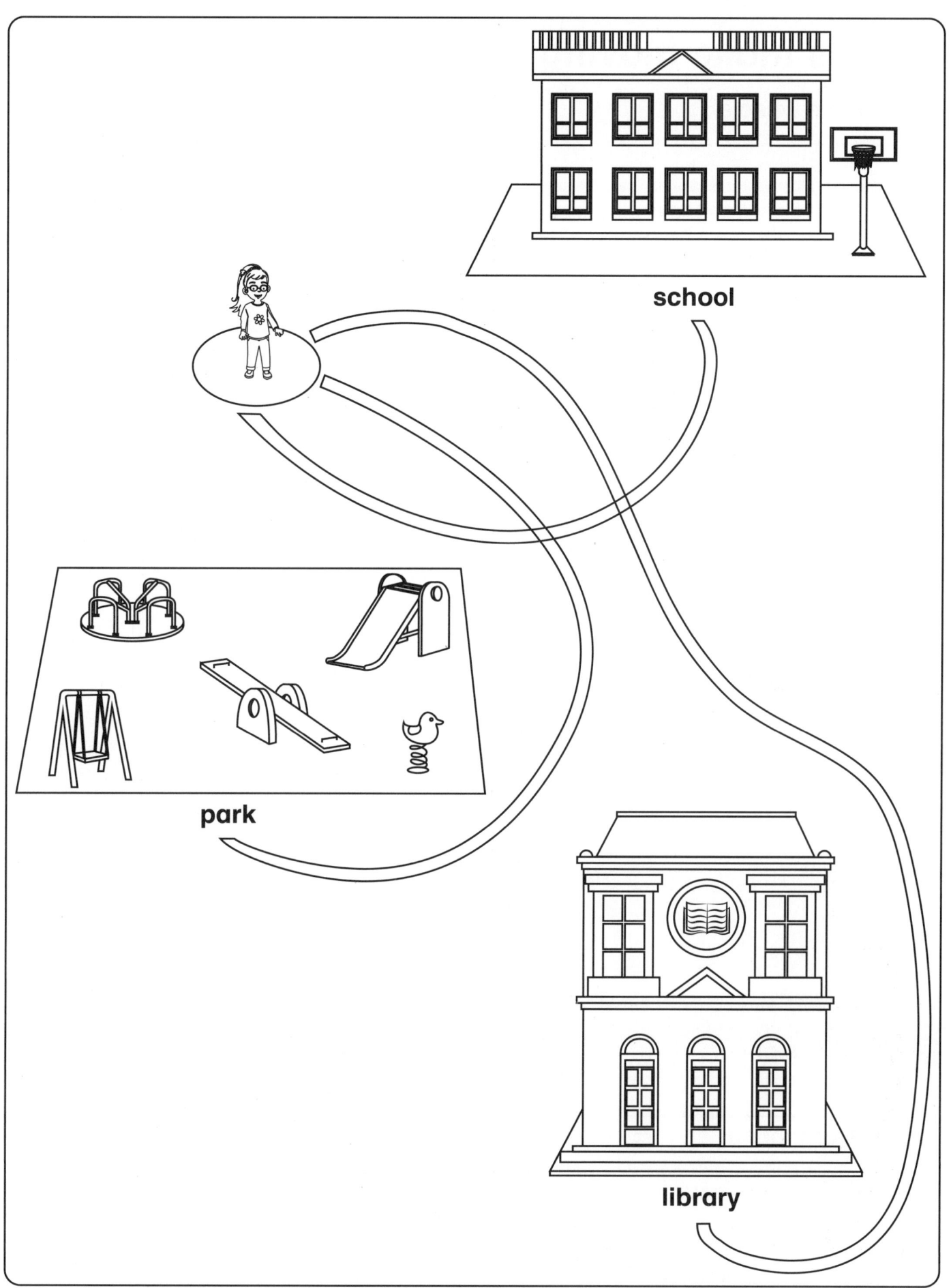

43

Wheels

Wheels make moving easy

❶ Draw the wheels.

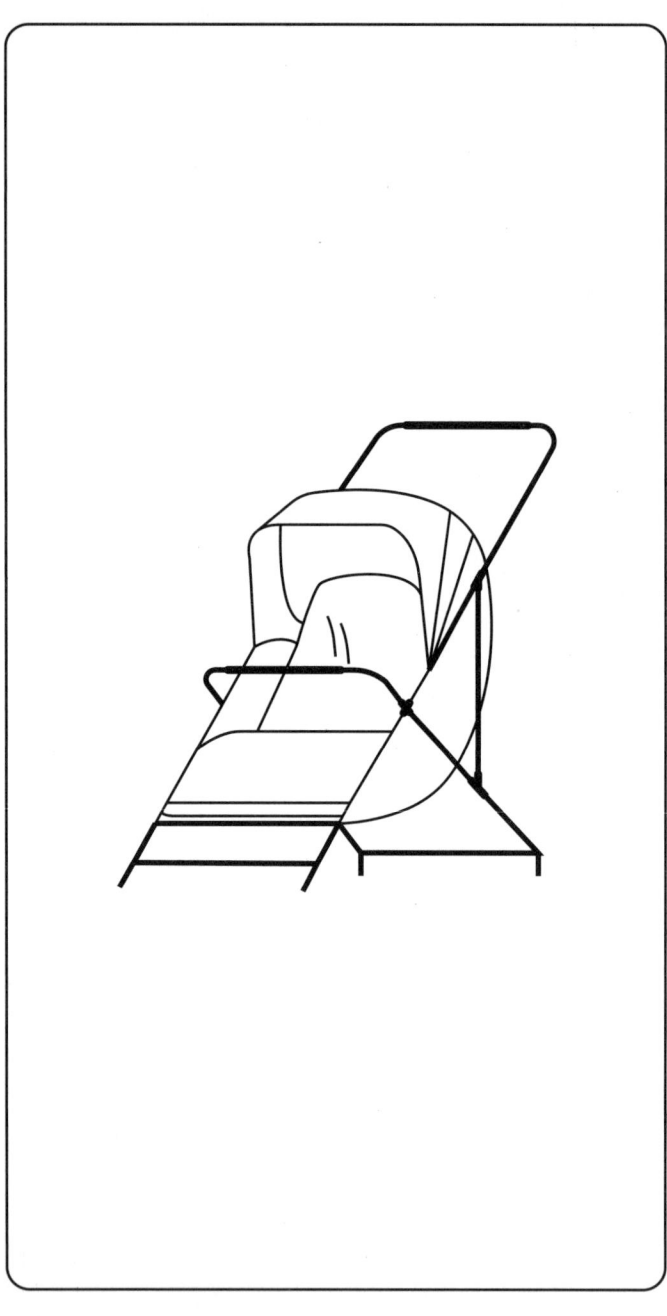

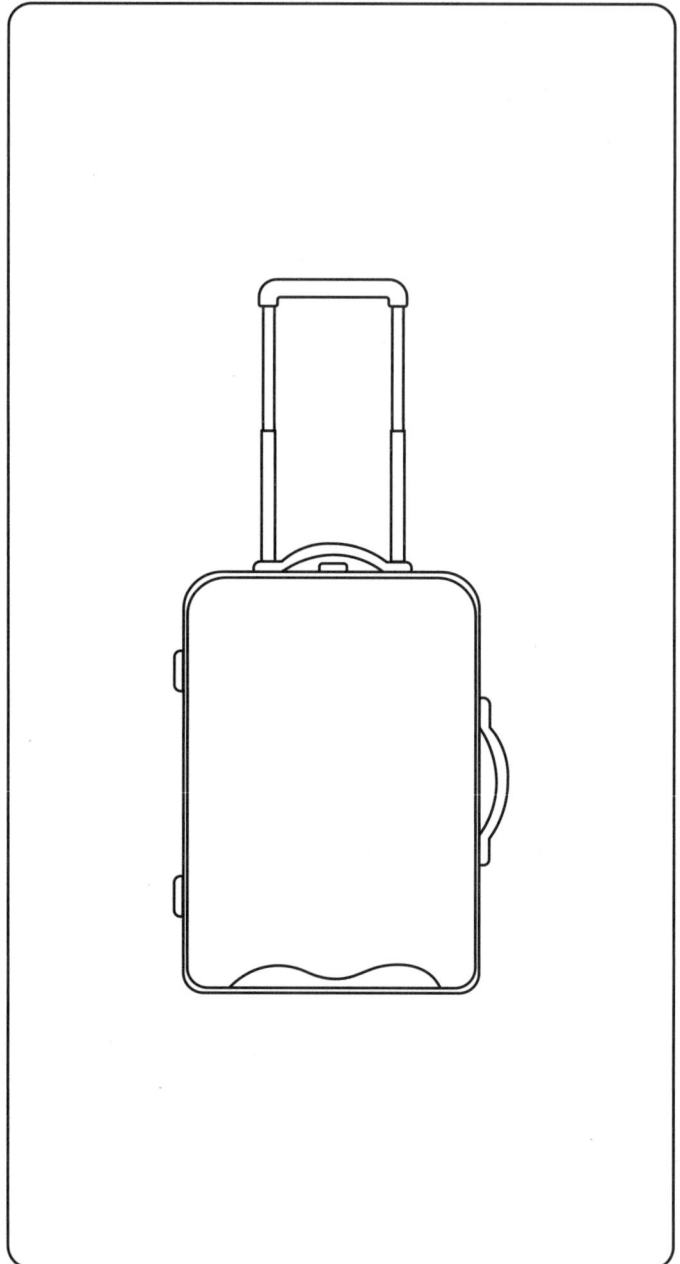

❷ Tick ✓ yes or no.

	Yes	No
Wheels are round.		
Wheels help you move.		
Skateboards have four wheels.		

Wheels help us travel

③ How many wheels? Colour in the chart.

Cars and lorries

Cars and lorries carry loads

❶ Draw lines to match the car or lorry to what it carries.

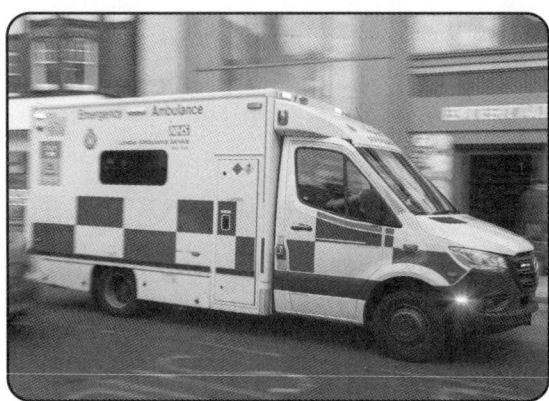

Cars and lorries make journeys

❷ Draw the journey of the car to the house.

Buses and trains

Buses and trains make long journeys

1 What is hidden in the picture?

　a) Colour in the key with one colour for each number.

　b) Use the key to colour the picture.

Key

1	2	3	4	5	6	7

48

Buses and trains use stations

2 Where do they stop? Draw lines to match the vehicles to where they stop.

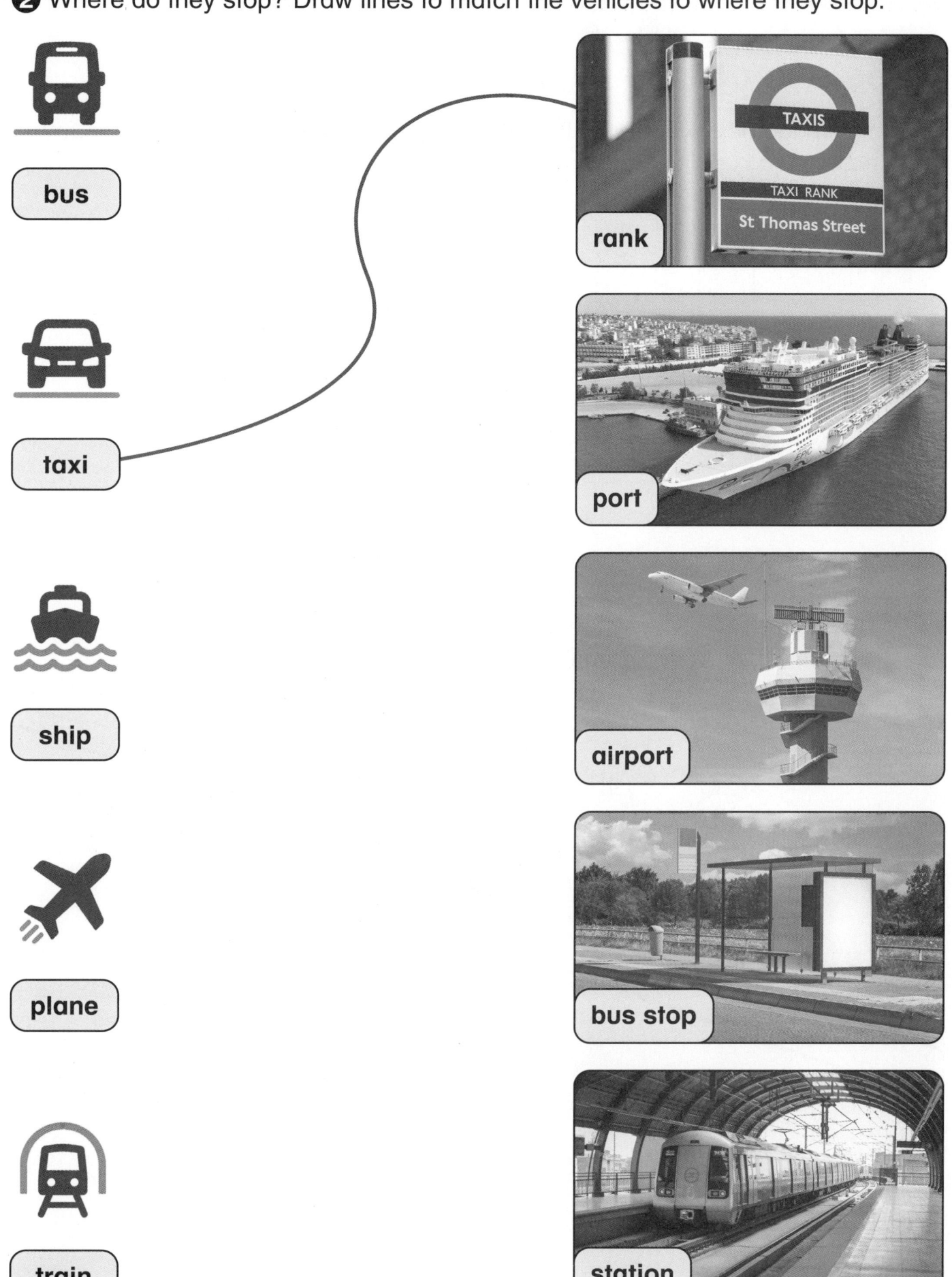

Colour

Maps use colour

❶ Look at page 52 of your Pupil Book. What colour are the places on the map? Complete the key.

countryside	
road	
town	
beach	

❷ Colour in the picture. Use the key.

Colours send messages

3 Colour in the:
- traffic lights
- steps
- green man.

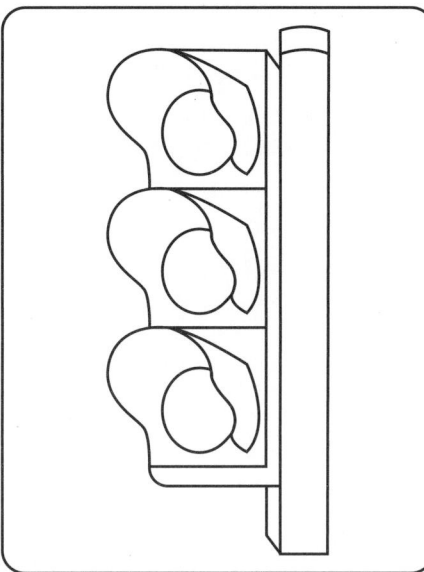
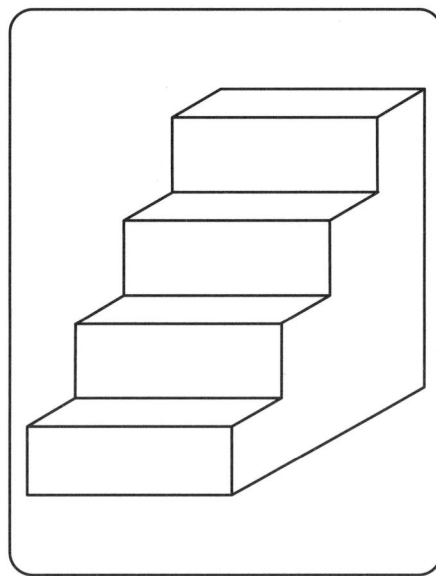

4 Draw and colour in two signs you see near your school.

Near and far

Places can be near or far

1 Circle the birds that are **near** the tree.

2 Colour in the T-shirts.

The girl has a yellow T-shirt.

The boy **far** from the girl has a blue T-shirt.

The boy **near** to the girl has a red T-shirt.

Maps show places near and far

3 Draw these places on the map:

a) a house and a tree **near** the bus.

b) a park and a shop **far** from the bus.

Low and high

Things can be low or high

1 Write 'high' or 'low'.

__high__

_____

_____

_____

Maps show places low and high

❷ Look at the room in a home.

Draw three things that are **high**.

Draw three things that are **low**.

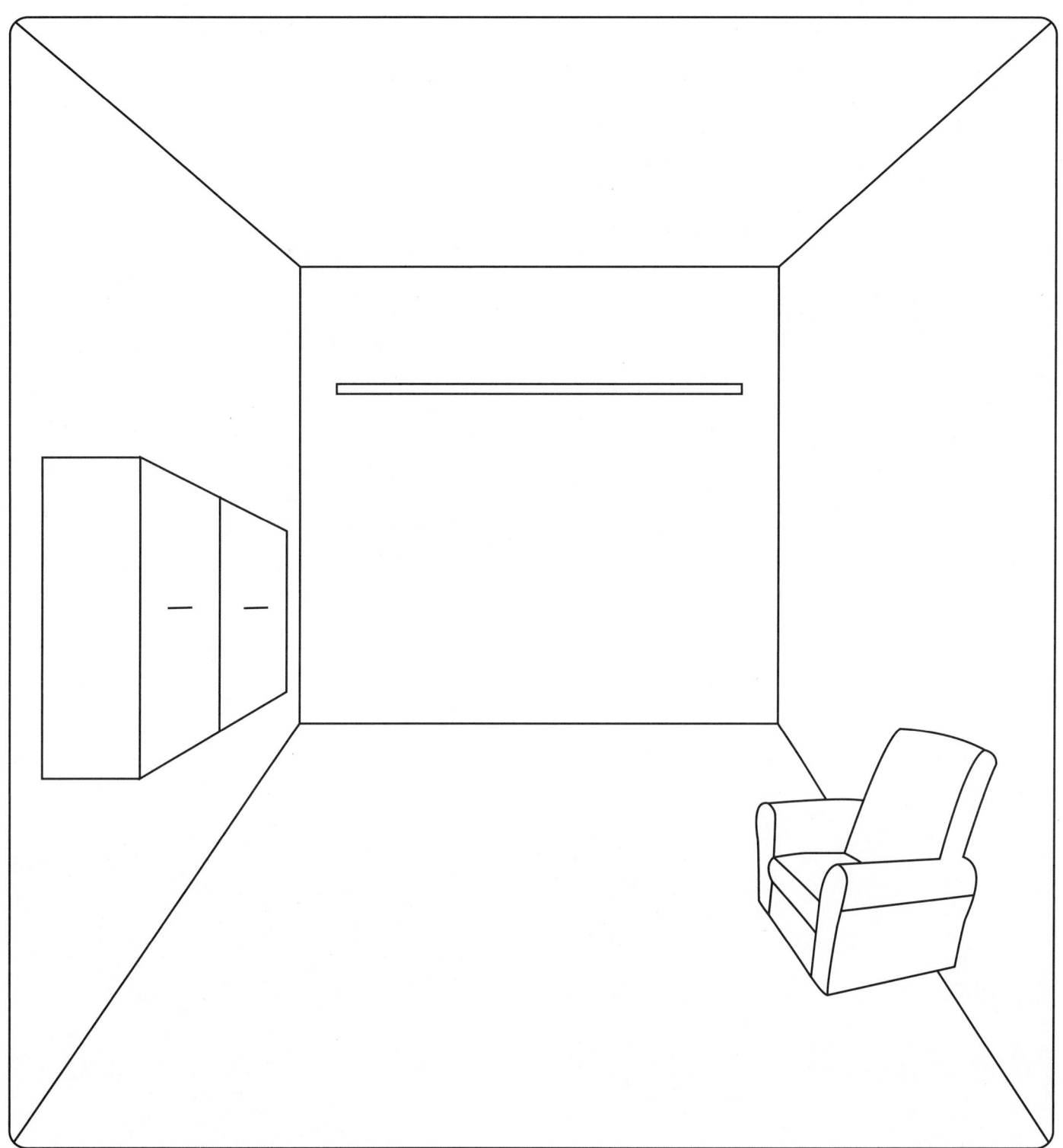

55

Signs

Signs tell us what to do

1 Yes or no? Colour the answer.

Can you ride a horse here?

Yes   No

Can you ride a bike here?

Yes   No

Can you make a fire here?

Yes   No

Can you walk across the road here?

Yes   No

Signs tell us messages

2 a) What do these signs tell us? Circle a word.

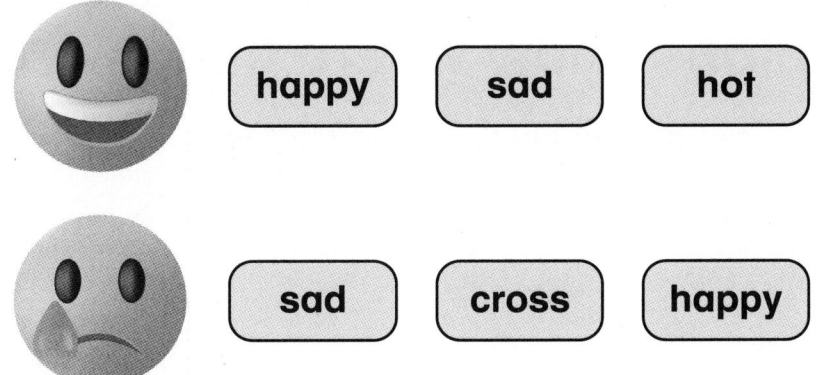

b) Draw a face sign to show how you feel now.

3 Draw two signs you may see in a park.

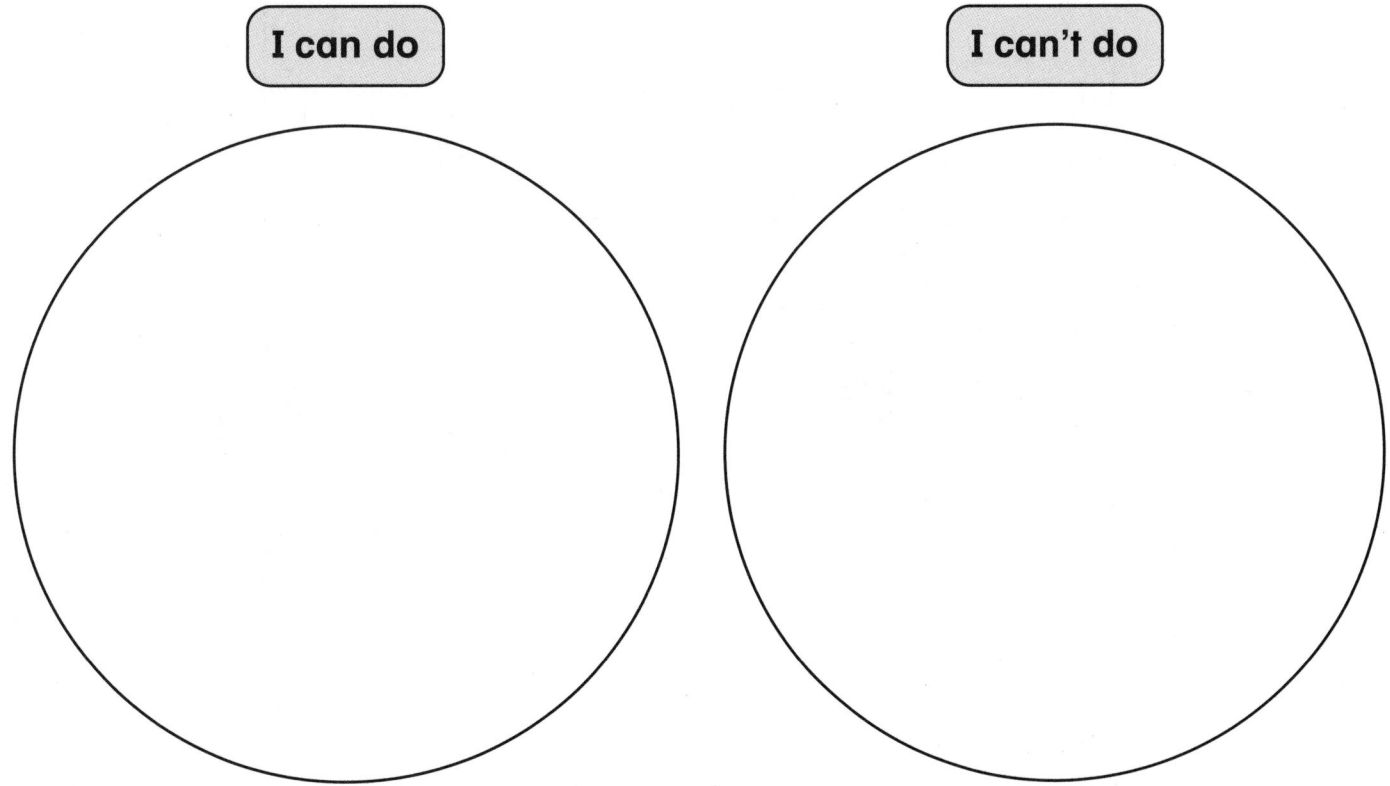

Maps and plans

Street maps and plans show where things are

1 Colour in the roads on the street map to show the way home.

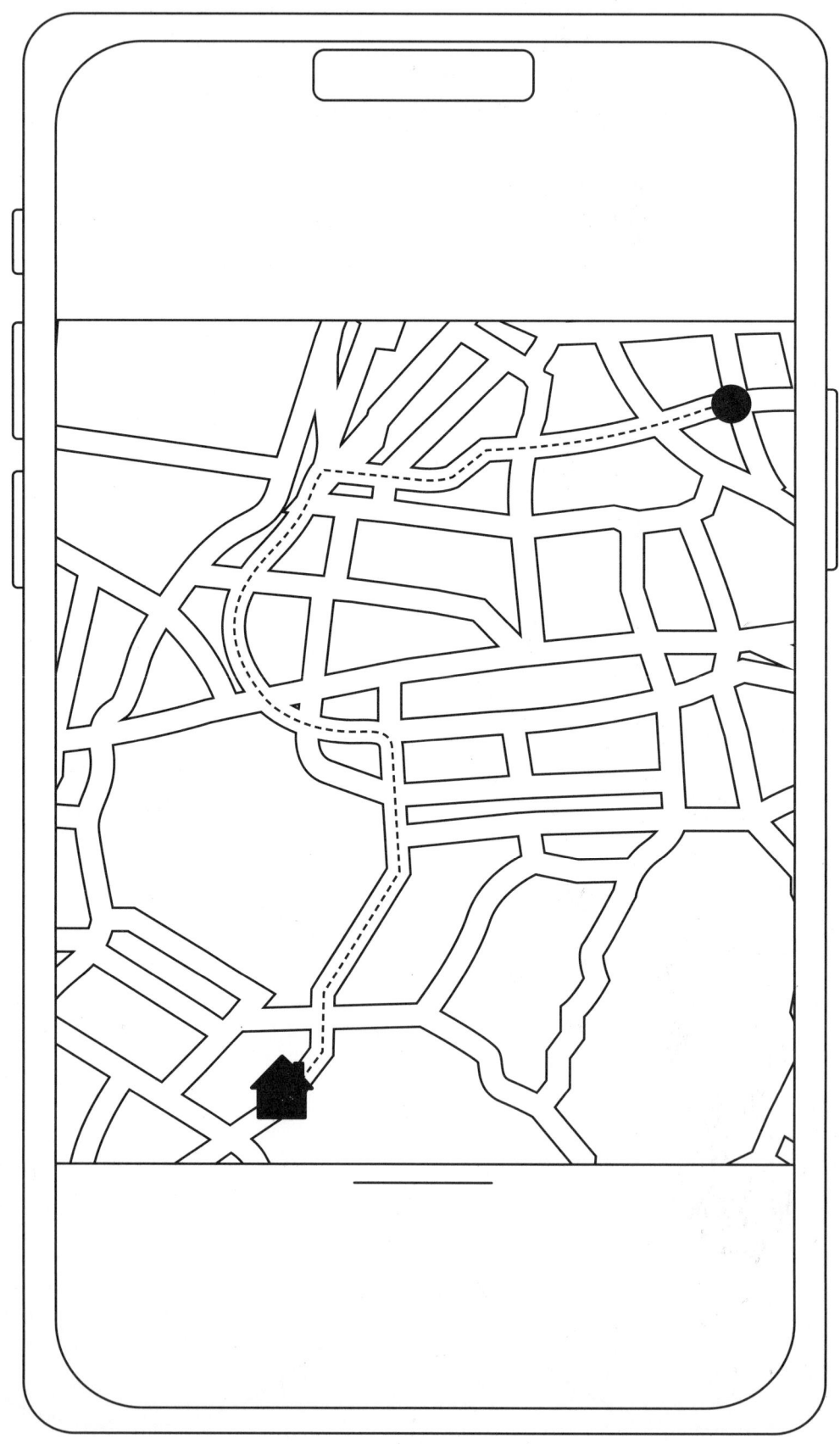

Maps and globes show where things are

❷ Join the numbers.

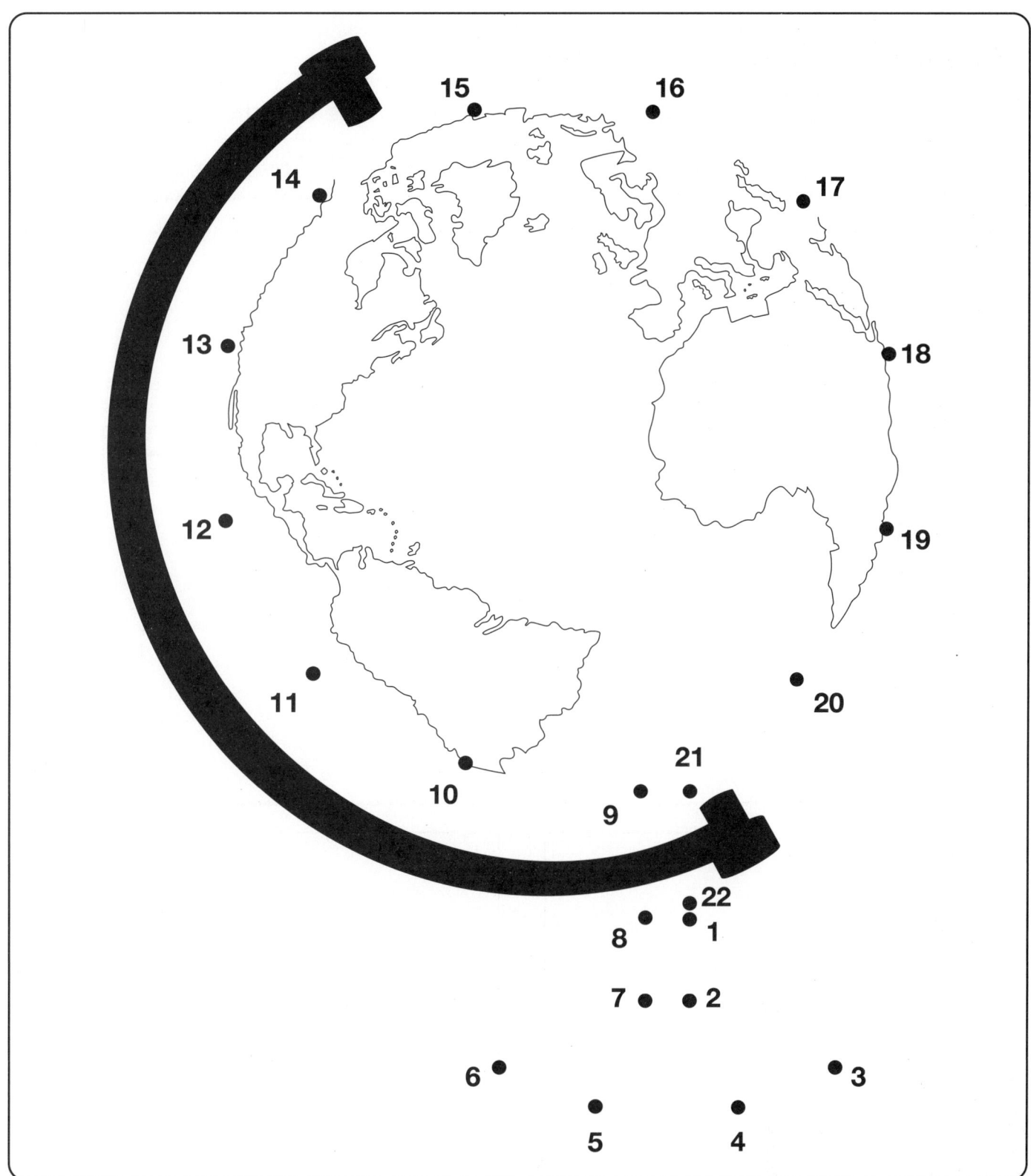

❸ Circle the best words.

This is a [globe] [glass].

It shows [the moon] [Planet Earth].

Our world

We must care for the world

❶ How can you care for the world? Choose one of these and draw a sign.

| Plant trees | Pick up litter | Make a garden | Save the soil |

This is the United Kingdom

2 Add words to the arrows on the compass.

north south east west

3 Colour the land green.

Notes

William Collins' dream of knowledge for all began with the publication of his first book in 1819.

A self-educated mill worker, he not only enriched millions of lives, but also founded a flourishing publishing house. Today, staying true to this spirit, Collins books are packed with inspiration, innovation and practical expertise.
They place you at the centre of a world of possibility and give you exactly what you need to explore it.

Published by Collins
An imprint of HarperCollins*Publishers*
The News Building, 1 London Bridge Street, London, SE1 9GF, UK

HarperCollins*Publishers*
Macken House, 39/40 Mayor Street Upper, Dublin 1, D01 C9W8, Ireland

Browse the complete Collins catalogue at
collins.co.uk

© HarperCollins*Publishers* Limited 2025
Maps © Collins Bartholomew 2025

10 9 8 7 6 5 4 3 2 1

ISBN 978-0-00-872834-2

All rights reserved. No part of this publication may be reproduced, stored in a retrieval system, or transmitted in any form by any means, electronic, mechanical, photocopying, recording or otherwise, without the prior written permission of the Publisher or a licence permitting restricted copying in the United Kingdom issued by the Copyright Licensing Agency Ltd, 5th Floor, Shackleton House, 4 Battle Bridge Lane, London, SE1 2HX.

British Library Cataloguing-in-Publication Data

A catalogue record for this publication is available from the British Library.

Author: Daphne Paizee
Publisher: Laura White
Product managers: Natasha Paul and Shelley Teasdale
Development editor: Judith Walters
Copyeditor: Fiona Watson
Proofreader: Charlotte Christensen
Cover designer and illustrator: Steve Evans
Internal illustrators: Jouve India Private Ltd and Ángeles Peinador, (Beehive Illustration)
Typesetter: David Jimenez
Production controllers: Alhady Ali and Katie Jean-Baptiste
Printed and bound in the UK by Martins the Printers

This book is produced from independently certified FSC™ paper to ensure responsible forest management.

For more information visit: www.harpercollins.co.uk/green
collins.co.uk/sustainability

Acknowledgements

The publishers gratefully acknowledge the permission granted to reproduce the copyright material in this book. Every effort has been made to trace copyright holders and to obtain their permission for the use of copyright material. The publishers will gladly receive any information enabling them to rectify any error or omission at the first opportunity.

All photos: Shutterstock.